World Health Organization
Regional Office for Europe
Copenhagen

WHO Regional Publications, European Series, No. 27

Drug abusers in prisons

Managing their health problems

Report on a WHO meeting

The Hague
16 –18 May 1988

ICP/ADA 515
Text editing by: Pamela M. Charlton

ISBN 92 890 1118 1
ISSN 0378-2255

PRINTED IN DENMARK

CONTENTS

Background and
purposes of the meeting

The proportion of drug abusers in the prison systems all over the world has grown enormously in recent decades. This has created a host of problems, not only for policy-makers, prison administrators and the drug abuse treatment system, but also for the drug-dependent prisoners themselves and their families. As a result of the advent of the acquired immunodeficiency syndrome (AIDS) epidemic and the steep rise in the rate of infection with human immunodeficiency virus (HIV) among drug abusers, the situation has become even more alarming.

The management of health problems among prison populations has increasingly had to concentrate on addiction problems and related ailments. In some countries, these pressures have led to a deterioration in the general health situation in prisons.

Although prison is far from the ideal setting for the treatment of drug dependence, a period of incarceration may facilitate some aspects of treatment and may help to motivate people to continue in therapy after their release.

An examination of the present situation and of current and alternative responses to the new demands has become urgent. For these reasons, the WHO Regional Office for Europe was pleased that the Ministry of Justice of the Netherlands was willing to collaborate in organizing a WHO meeting on the management of health problems of drug abusers in prisons.

The main purposes of the meeting were to bring together information from a number of countries on the management of the health problems of drug abusers in prisons, to exchange experience on relevant issues, to consider possible national and international research on the topic, and to draw up a report and recommendations

1

for wide distribution to prison and health authorities. The agenda covered the following topics:

— the administration and organization of health care for drug abusers in prisons;

— the identification of drug abusers in prisons;

— health care measures for drug abusers on admission;

— the treatment of drug dependence after detoxification;

— the special nature of drug treatment in prisons, voluntary and non-voluntary;

— other health problems, particularly HIV infection, AIDS and suicidal behaviour;

— research questions and priorities;

— conclusions and recommendations.

The meeting was held in The Hague from 16 to 18 May 1988 and brought together 19 experts in the fields of psychiatry, psychology, sociology, social work, law and medicine from 10 European countries and the United States (see Annex 2 for a list of participants). A number of the participants had prepared working papers specifically for the meeting. Professor Casselman, in his capacity as WHO consultant, had drawn up a report covering five European countries, on offenders in prison with problems related to the abuse of illicit drugs. Some additional general background documentation was provided by the Pompidou Group[a] of the Council of Europe. These working papers are listed in Annex 1. Together with the discussions, and an earlier study by Casselman (2), this documentation provided the basis for this report.

Dr P. Lens, Chief Medical Officer at the Ministry of Justice, welcomed the participants to the meeting on behalf of the Minister of Justice. Mr C. Goos, Scientist, Abuse of Psychoactive Drugs, welcomed the participants to the meeting on behalf of the Regional

---

[a] The Pompidou Group is an intergovernmental working group consisting of 19 out of the 21 Member States of the Council of Europe. It is concerned with several aspects of drug problems, with the exception of drug production and primary prevention. This Group has organized two seminars on the role of the criminal justice system in responding to the problems of drug abusers (1).

Director of the WHO Regional Office for Europe. Mr Goos expressed his gratitude to the Ministry of Justice for hosting the meeting on the premises of the Ministry and for the valuable assistance that Dr P.A. Roorda, Dr Lens, Mr L.H. Erkelens and other personnel of the Ministry had given in the preparation of the meeting. Dr Lens was elected Chairman of the meeting. Mr H. van Vliet assisted in the preparation of this report.

Administration and organization

In Europe, a certain basic level of health care is provided for every inmate. In general there is at least some form of medical attention for offenders entering prison. Nevertheless, the administration and organization of the health care systems differ between countries as do the level of specialization in detecting drug users and the methods of dealing with them.

Casselman's study *(2)* covered Belgium, Ireland, Italy, the Netherlands and Sweden. It shows that judicial authorities and, more specifically, prison administrations have the main responsibility for organizing health care in prisons, whereas the health authorities and health professionals play only a secondary role. The five countries studied by Casselman have a variety of systems of organization. Nurses and general practitioners are usually available, and sometimes a consultant psychiatrist. Staff who give general medical care or specialized drug assistance may either be members of the prison staff or come from outside the prison. Drug assistance staff who are members of the prison staff are usually professionals, while external staff may also be volunteers. The possible lack of expertise in dealing with drugs inside some prison systems may be an incentive for seeking external counsellors.

Identification of drug abusers in prisons

The first step in dealing with the various health problems of drug abusers in prisons is to identify drug abusers among the new admissions. On a more general level, the nature and extent of drug-related problems in the prison system need to be estimated.

Individual Identification

Most frequently the inmate comes to the prison already labelled as a drug user/abuser/addict. This label is based on some evidence presented to the administration of the justice system (e.g. self-reporting, needle marks, typical offences such as pharmacy burglary, possession of injection equipment, lifestyle, intoxication, withdrawal symptoms, urine or blood testing). On the other hand, some offenders (e.g. some professional dealers, ex-abusers and others) do not actually use drugs, but claim to do so in order to obtain special or better treatment or alternatives to imprisonment, intended for or more easily granted to drug-dependent inmates.

If a new inmate is presented or presents him/herself as a drug abuser, the physician may often only gather a little more case history data. More attention should be paid, however, to gathering detailed information on actual and past drug use, the nature and patterns of use (often polydrug use), the type and degree of dependence, individual and psychosocial characteristics, and so on. Inmates may be screened for drug dependence and psychiatric disorders, using for example the Addiction Severity Index (ASI) and the Diagnostic Interview Scheme (DIS). Experience with these instruments has been gathered in the United States and shows

5

that they can be helpful for obtaining a more precise diagnosis. Some European countries are starting to use them on a more regular basis.

Some inmates are not known to be drug users when admitted to prison. Their identification is desirable, however, if a more appropriate enforcement of criminal sanctions and more adequate health care and treatment can be achieved as a result. Conversely, care should be taken not to identify occasional users as drug dependent or addicted, as this can have negative effects such as stigmatization, marginalization and increased drug use. Some subgroups of drug users, however, should be investigated systematically, e.g. injectors, as a group at high risk for HIV infection. Blood screening has recently been introduced in most countries for some groups at risk. The use of screening in prison populations, the number of HIV-infected inmates and the provision of information on HIV and AIDS to inmates and prison staff vary widely between countries.

Incidence and Prevalence Estimates

In several European countries, attempts have been made to identify the nature and extent of drug-related problems in prison, on admission or at other times, by using repeated searches or continuous registration. Identification on a more general level is important for developing policies to deal with the growing number of drug abusers in prison. In some countries, systematic registration systems are only in the planning stage, as part of a more sophisticated automatization of data collection. Regularly repeated day-prevalence registration is the most frequently used system. Incidence data are less frequently available, and specific surveys (using questionnaires and/or urine testing) are relatively rare. As a consequence, information on the nature of problems related to illicit drug use among inmates is limited.

Casselman noted a relationship between the prevalence of drug users inside the prison system and the level of health care: countries with a low prevalence of drug abusers in prison tended to have a lower level of general and specialized health care. The situation in a southern European country such as Spain, however, contradicts these findings: in a number of prisons, especially in centres of drug use such as Madrid, Barcelona and Bilbao, many drug-dependent inmates have little medical assistance of any type.

6

The results Casselman obtained in the different countries are not scientifically comparable: the research designs and the type of data collected differ from one country to another. According to the latest figures, the prevalence of drug users inside the prison systems in the five countries he studied ranges from one third to one tenth of the total prison population. In France — not included in Casselman's research — about a quarter to one third of the prison population, depending on the region, have drug-dependence problems. The general trend in these countries shows an increase in prevalence over the last few years, but the starting point and the configuration of the increase vary from country to country. An important overall trend is the general change from opiate to polydrug use, including alcohol and benzodiazepines.

A factor to be considered in interpreting the available data is the different detention rates between the five countries studied by Casselman. At 1 September 1984, the detention rates per 100 000 inhabitants were 66 for Belgium, 44.1 for Ireland, 76.1 for Italy, 33 for the Netherlands and 48 for Sweden (3). Moreover, the specific detention policies for drug abusers in these countries are also different.

Another basic problem is the widespread confusion of terms when drug-related problems are presented. The inadequate use of terminology in general, and particularly within the administration of the judicial system, results in faulty problem assessment and intervention strategies. Concepts such as drug use, misuse, abuse, intoxication, overdose, dependence and addiction are often mixed up. It is not always evident what kinds of psychoactive drug are involved (e.g. illicit or prescribed drugs, including abusively prescribed psychoactive drugs or not). The distinction between abusers and dealer/abusers on the one hand, and traffickers/non-abusers on the other is not always clear. The methods of gathering the information also differ: most frequently the central prison administration asks the prison directors to provide data. The involvement of medical or welfare staff, mostly not specialized, is not always clearly specified.

Health care measures
for drug abusers
on admission

In most countries, drug withdrawal is an inevitable consequence of detention, although medical assistance is provided. Casselman's study shows that in Belgium and Ireland — countries with a low drug prevalence in prison populations — drug withdrawal is mainly limited to traditional withdrawal methods. In countries with a high prevalence, other options are frequently offered; very often other drugs are prescribed. This option is generally started as a preventive measure and based mainly on the information given by the inmate. The prescription is sometimes continued at the inmate's request and may include methadone maintenance treatment. Inmates with drug-related problems may also be transferred to a special section (prison hospital, psychiatric ward) for withdrawal or further treatment if available. Although great efforts are made to ensure that prisons are a drug-free environment, there are drugs in most prisons, both prescribed and illicit. Prescribing psychoactive drugs (including benzodiazepines) to inmates can be valid medical practice. Furthermore, sleeping pills, as well as an illicit drug such as cannabis, can have a relaxing influence on the attitude of inmates towards prison staff. In some cases a black market in prescribed drugs develops, but a black market and trafficking inside prisons might be a symptom of deficient medical care. Intensive medical care, including the prescription of drugs, may also have a positive effect on the management of such problems.

Detoxification is not the only health care measure necessary for drug abusers on admission. The need for psychosocial crisis intervention for inmates with drug-related problems is sometimes more urgent than any other care. Crisis intervention, of course, should not be confined to the admission period; it should be available if necessary at any time and to all inmates. It is important to mention, however, that health care measures on admission are often limited to traditional detoxification. Another short-term goal on admission is the screening for and treatment of secondary drug problems such as diseases associated with drug dependence.

Treatment of drug dependence in prison

After drug abusers are identified and, if necessary, detoxified, they may receive drug abuse treatment, in conjunction with, or instead of, completing their prison term. In most European countries, prison authorities are convinced that "normal" detention is an inadequate option for addicted drug users, especially when they are admitted to the prison system in large numbers. The countries studied by Casselman *(2)* reported various ways of coping with the growing number of dependent drug users.

Treatment of Primary Drug-dependence Problems

The treatment of drug-related health problems can be separated into the treatment of the primary health problems (drug dependence and related problems) and the secondary health problems often associated with the illegal and unhealthy circumstances related to drug use, such as physical and mental deterioration, and disorders including hepatitis, pneumonia and HIV/AIDS in particular.

Casselman reports that the low prevalence countries in his study, Belgium and Ireland, have a less well developed drug assistance structure in their prisons. The same is true for Spain, which has many drug-dependent inmates in detention. High prevalence countries, such as the Netherlands and Sweden, as well as the Federal Republic of Germany, have a wide range of procedures for

10

dealing with imprisoned drug users, from counselling inside prison to full-scale therapeutic community programmes outside.[a]

In the northern European low prevalence countries, and in southern Europe, the drug abuse treatment structure appears to be more medically oriented, while the northern European high prevalence countries generally operate with multidisciplinary teams of physicians, psychologists and social workers. Most countries admit, however, that prison is not the ideal place for drug-dependence treatment.

The following options for treatment after sentencing or detoxification can be distinguished:

— drug-free treatment in prison in line with the therapeutic community approach;

— other treatment procedures in prison (often limited because in a number of European countries prison sentences for drug users last months rather than years);

— treatment outside prison as an alternative to detention, or after detention, possibly in combination with early or temporary release.

In each of these situations drug users need to be motivated to make use of the options offered, and to carry out the necessary arrangements.

Motivation to Enter Treatment

Incarcerating drug-dependent persons does not solve their drug problems, and prison is not a therapeutic environment. Moreover, detention is generally very boring, although for many drug abusers imprisonment is much easier than going into and staying in treatment. They know the rules and have learned very quickly to survive within or just outside these rules. For example, the prospect of living through four months of detention is often less frightening than the idea of living through up to two years of drug-free treatment. Besides, drug-dependent inmates can put pressure

---

[a] A therapeutic community is a specific treatment modality, originally developed in the United Kingdom and the United States, in which a very intensive community regime is applied to all the participants in the programme.

on other drug abusers not to go into treatment and thus violate the implicit rules of the drug scene, often set by drug dealers both inside and outside prisons.

It is practically impossible to measure motivation. Almost every drug abuser is motivated to end the misery of being a drug-dependent prisoner, but drug abusers often tend to overestimate their endurance and to underestimate the difficulties of serious treatment. Lack of motivation is easier to detect, especially when the words and actions of the drug abuser are contradictory. Signs that suggest a positive prognosis include:

— the restoration of family relations

— the completion of professional schooling

— experience with regular work.

Signs that suggest a negative prognosis include:

— friends and family disapproving of treatment on entry

— having a drug-dependent boy- or girlfriend

— having a history of non-compliance with appointments

— drug use or dependence on any prescribed drug during detention.

Too often being motivated is considered to be a defined status instead of a process, with many ups and downs. As a consequence it is much easier to destroy motivation than help it to develop and grow. The prejudices of prison authorities, fellow-inmates, relatives and drug counsellors towards addicts can have a devastating influence on the motivational process. Therefore, it seems important to motivate those entering treatment by:

— providing them with correct factual information;

— arranging a live preview of the treatment;

— ensuring the effective cooperation of all persons and processes involved in the preparation for treatment and the treatment itself.

A surprising amount of harm can be done when these conditions are neglected: the drug abuser may feel cheated and drop out. It is impossible to learn from written information how it feels to participate in a therapeutic group session; this has to be experienced. Group sessions for dependent inmates and a visit to the therapeutic programme are helpful. On the other hand, drug counsellors who carry out motivational tasks should be well informed about the realities of prison life; ignorant outsiders can easily destroy the delicate balance of motivation for drug treatment. Ex-abusers with prison experience can be positive role models for abusers who are destined to enter treatment; they know what it is all about and they have demonstrated their ability to stay drug free. The missionary project in the Malmö area of Sweden serves as an example of this motivational process.

Getting drug-dependent inmates into treatment, especially outside the prison system, depends on many often rather complicated procedures involving many people. Therefore it is reasonable, as part of the establishment of objective criteria for furthering the motivational process, to develop checklists to establish smooth procedures without omissions.

Not all prison inmates are drug abusers and when much attention is given specifically to drug abusers, non-abusers can feel neglected and cause trouble. For example, they may be motivated to use drugs themselves in order to get more staff attention, medical care and rehabilitation programmes. The pressure on drug-free inmates to start using drugs in prison is a serious problem in many places. Adequate protection for non-users should therefore be available.

Counselling in Prison by Outsiders

A possibly very fruitful way of improving prison care is to call on the help of professionals from outside the prison system. This is done, for example, in the Federal Republic of Germany, the Netherlands and Sweden. In Sweden, the missionary project already mentioned works with ex-drug-abusers to motivate drug-dependent inmates to apply for a drug treatment programme when they are released on parole. In the Netherlands, prison work by parole officers and volunteers from outside the prison is a long-standing tradition. The influx of drug users since the mid-1970s has increased the involvement of outsiders, particularly through the ambulatory treatment institutions (CADs)[a]. In France, work is under way to facilitate access by external institutions to build a bridge for those who want to enter treatment after they leave prison

---

[a] *Consultatie-bureau voor Alcohol en Drugs.*

and to help drug abusers cope with the fear of life outside prison. This access also increases the outside institutions' awareness of the changes that are taking place in the diverse, heterogeneous and volatile drug milieu, since the prison system is generally the first institution in society to be affected. In the Federal Republic of Germany, external drug counsellors specifically concentrate on motivating drug-dependent inmates to undergo treatment in a therapeutic community or other kind of programme after leaving prison.

Federal Republic of Germany

The first attempts to introduce drug assistance in the Federal Republic of Germany date back to the late 1960s and early 1970s. As in other northern European countries a progression can be seen, going from the inability of the established assistance system to cope with the new problems, through volunteer and self-help initiatives, to a highly specialized and professionalized drug treatment system in the late 1970s.

Traditional professionalism in particular has created a distance between the drug abuser and the counsellor. The approach used by most drug-treatment and drug-counselling centres can only be described as waiting: the drug user has to come to the counsellor and not the other way around. Although outreach and easy access projects existed in the late 1970s (e.g. streetwork and drop-in centres), such projects were atypical of the professional assistance to drug abusers in the Federal Republic of Germany.

At the end of the 1970s, the public in the Federal Republic of Germany became aware of drug problems as a threat to society. Drug deaths (by overdose) were counted and the number of addicts (mainly heroin users) was expected to rise sharply. The drug-abuse assistance system tried to counter these developments through the expansion and variety of approaches. The police and the judiciary reacted by attempting to destroy the local drug enclaves by arresting drug abusers and sentencing them to prison. The effects on the prison system were dramatic. At the beginning of the 1970s the proportion of drug abusers within the total prison population was minimal. According to Kaiser et al. *(4)*, at the end of the 1970s about 10–15% of the 48 200 prisoners in the Federal Republic of Germany were drug-dependent. Three years later Kindermann *(5)* estimated that almost one third of the prisoners in the Federal Republic of Germany and Berlin (West) were probably addicted to opiates.

14

The Federal Republic of Germany's prison system was thus confronted with a problem of unprecedented size. This often led to an admission of helplessness and, in some cases, drug professionals were called on for help. These professionals on the other hand saw their work (and their demands for public funding) endangered by the trend that a growing proportion of their potential clients were becoming practically unreachable because of imprisonment. Eventually, more drug-abuse assistance centres decided to make offers of help to imprisoned drug users, and prison administrations became increasingly willing to let these centres take responsibility for counselling on drug abuse in prisons.

The introduction of such counselling in a number of prisons was accompanied by a debate about its pros and cons. Two opposing viewpoints were apparent: the rejection of such activities in prison, and a more pragmatic approach. The objectors were mainly against the criminalization and imprisonment of drug abusers and opposed to any cooperation. They argued that active cooperation with the prison system would not reduce the criminalization of drug abusers. In fact, drug counsellors would provide the judicial system with an excuse to imprison even more drug abusers, because professional counselling would take place inside the prisons. A second argument was that these counsellors would help stabilize the system by filling a gap. As qualified drug treatment personnel, they would supplement the chronically under-staffed social services inside the prisons. A third argument often used was the lack of free will among drug-dependent inmates. Imprisoned drug abusers were stated to be unable to decide for themselves whether they wanted to participate in treatment after prison. Any decision would be influenced by its likely effect on getting out of prison; therefore, their wish to enter treatment would not be real or well founded. Under these conditions, objectors stated that drug counselling could not and should not be carried out inside prisons.

The pragmatists on the other hand, argued that contact with and counselling of drug-dependent individuals should take place whenever and wherever possible. Counselling drug abusers in prison differs from other forms of outreach only in the location. It comes down to the question of either leaving drug-dependent inmates to their own fate, or trying to supply support and care. External counsellors would anyway have to limit their activities to the drug problems of the inmates and associated matters. General problems of the penal system and associated inmate problems would not be part of the relation between inmates and their drug counsellor. The drug user will always be ambivalent about his/her dependency. External pressure is necessary to help motivate the abuser to give up drugs. In this way, a stay in prison can become meaningful if access to treatment is made available.

The judiciary and the prison authorities reacted differently to the influx of external drug counsellors into the prison system, especially in those prisons where external counsellors worked on their own initiative without waiting to be summoned into the prison, causing them to be rejected and ostracized. Sometimes even the goal of referring drug abusers for community treatment was considered a provocation and external counsellors were accused of helping prisoners to escape. For many prison employees, the activities of the external counsellors were primarily an extra burden and a disturbance of the routine: prisoners' applications for counselling had to be administered, prisoners had to be brought to and from counselling sessions, and counsellors had to be admitted to the prison. Prison social workers and psychologists sometimes envied external counsellors and many expressed competitive feelings towards them. Further, they thought the working conditions of their community colleagues, who only spent part of their time inside, were much better than their own; they felt their flexibility and the opportunity to avoid bureaucracy were more effective and regarded their degree of independence from the judiciary as a privilege.

Facing such resistance and problems, the judiciary and the prison authorities developed another approach by offering the external counsellors better integration into the prison system, easier admission, freedom of movement in prison, upgraded status and access to important papers such as prison files. This improved the external counsellors' working conditions, enhanced their cooperation with prison staff and generally improved the working climate. But there were also prisons where outside counsellors were always welcomed with open arms, and were given resources far beyond the minimal requirements, such as keys so that they could come and go freely, and rooms for counselling sessions and for completing their paperwork. There are even counsellors who spend their entire working day in prison although they are still employees of an external institution. Such positions inside prisons have a number of advantages for counsellors which include being better informed and having more intensive contacts in prison. In short, they belong.

16

Nevertheless, the external counsellor should never belong to the prison and to the institutionalized judicial system. Particularly in the eyes of their clients or potential clients external counsellors should keep some distance from the prison institution; their effectiveness depends not only on their professional qualifications as a drug counsellor, but also on their independence from the traditional prison system. It is this ability to keep at a distance that qualifies them as a trustworthy partner from the drug user's point of view. Most external drug counsellors engage in a critical and reserved cooperation with the judicial system. The *Verband ambulanter Behandlungsstellen für Suchtkranke/Drogen-abhängige* (Society for Outpatient Care of Addicts/Drug Dependents) has established a set of rules as guidance for this specific type of work:

— nonbureaucratic access without the need for special permission to visit;

— no control of the counsellors (such as by body searches);

— no control of the papers necessary for treatment (files, case summaries, applications, etc.);

— all sessions between a counsellor and an inmate should be confidential, without the presence of a guard, and without a time limit;

— rooms should be made available where one-to-one and group sessions can take place;

— guaranteed support by prison employees as required (doctors' certificates, etc.).

The special nature
of treatment of
drug abusers within prisons

The main difference between treatment outside and treatment within the prison system is the constraint and coercion that being in prison entails. Every step in the treatment process within prison, from motivation to aftercare, is extorted in a way by the very nature of the prison system: inmates are not physically free, as a rule they are coerced into living a drug-free life, and they are circumstantially forced to think about their drug use and about being drug-free. To a certain degree, this coercion can be and is being used to motivate the inmate to enter treatment for drug dependence. Nevertheless these treatment procedures will be considered here as voluntary.

The word non-voluntary is used when treatment is imposed as an instrument of the judicial authorities, whether executed within or outside the prison system.

Voluntary Treatment

Of the five countries studied by Casselman, only the Netherlands and Sweden provide specific drug treatment facilities inside prisons. They also provide treatment alternatives outside prisons as do Ireland and Italy. In France — not part of the study — several special facilities for drug users are available in some prisons.

France
Since 1838, a sharp line has traditionally been drawn in France between offenders with psychiatric disorders and other normal offenders. People dependent on alcohol and drugs are considered

to be fundamentally psychiatric patients. In effect, this means that it is forbidden to accommodate psychiatric — including drug-dependent — inmates with normal inmates, and to treat the former against their will. In many prisons there are mental sections, but inmates cannot be obliged to be treated there. According to the Law of 31 December 1970, the basic French anti-drug law, drug users should be given the choice between continuation of the criminal procedures or entering detoxification and treatment but, because of technical difficulties and the interpretation of the law as it applies to drug use, this law is rarely used to get people into treatment.

The first time special attention was paid to drug users in prison was in the late 1970s, when their numbers increased considerably. The creation in 1977 of regional penitentiary psychomedical services — aimed at inmates with psychiatric disorders in general — enabled special attention to be given to drug users. A particular problem with including addiction as a mental illness was that about two thirds of the drug abusers entering prison were already offenders who had originally belonged to the group of normal offenders, before they began to abuse drugs thus becoming labelled as mentally ill. It was not until 1986, however, that the *antennes specialisées* for drug users were brought into operation: these special teams consisted of physicians, nurses, social workers and educators; they started in four prisons on an experimental basis and had expanded to 16 prisons by the end of 1988.

Ireland
In Ireland, Section 28 of the Misuse of Drugs Act of 1977, and its amendment in 1984, include the possibility of organizing specific treatment units for drug abusers, but no specific units have yet been set up. It is possible, however, for some prisoners to be granted temporary release in order to attend the Coolemine therapeutic community, which provides several residential and ambulatory programmes.

Italy
In Italy, the relevant legal position is Paragraph 47*bis* of Law No. 297 of 21 June 1985. This law makes it possible for convicted drug users who have been sentenced to less than 2½ years of imprisonment (3 years for juveniles), to undergo treatment instead of detention. This has been introduced to increase the treatment

options for drug users in both residential and ambulatory care. It is based on a contract between the person concerned and the treatment centre. If the drug user interrupts the treatment or avoids undergoing it, an order of imprisonment will be issued and the preceding period of treatment will not count as part of the total initial prison sentence. In any event, a person may benefit only once from this measure. Another treatment possibility is offered by Law No. 532 of 12 August 1982. Drug users, imprisoned but awaiting trial, can remain at home or in other private places (under house arrest), or in a public health institution instead of staying in custody. Many drug users have been sent to therapeutic communities under this law, and provisional liberty is often granted more easily in order not to interrupt a course of treatment.

Netherlands
In the Netherlands, many drug-dependent inmates are serving short prison sentences and as only a few are motivated for treatment, many do not receive treatment in prison. Some prisons have, however, developed special drug-free units that offer treatment facilities, and help prepare inmates for treatment outside prison. This is mostly organized through the assistance of specialized ambulatory services based outside, but often operating in the prison location.

Treatment outside the prison (but as part of the prison system) is made possible by Paragraph 47 of the national prison regulations. This Paragraph offers the opportunity for the admission of inmates into a hospital in case of "mental illness or serious or contagious disease". This has been interpreted to include drug dependence. A number of treatment centres are willing to accept drug abusers during their detention on the condition that the prison administration is informed if treatment is interrupted. Prisoners can make use of Paragraph 47 once they have served half of their sentence. Treatment usually continues after the end of the prison sentence.

In 1979, two experimental projects for drug abusers were started in the remand homes of Amsterdam and Rotterdam. In Amsterdam, a separate wing was established and staffed by specialists recruited from the Amsterdam outpatient drug treatment centres. In 1982, the experiment was converted into a regular drug treatment programme for 12 inmates, increased to 24 in 1984. In Rotterdam, the experimental programme was introduced step by step, partly because no separate unit was available in the beginning. Now a special drug unit is in operation for about 30 inmates with drug-related problems. Trained prison staff and staff from an outpatient centre are in charge and control measures (urine testing, searching after visits, etc.) are part of the programme. In some other cities, outpatient centres have set up projects to provide information and counselling inside prisons. In The Hague such a project, gradually developing into a more structured programme, has been in operation in the youth remand home De Sprang since 1981.

Sweden

In Sweden, just as in the Netherlands, the stay in prison is relatively short for a large number of drug-dependent inmates. This puts a severe constraint on treatment attempts during this period and emphasizes the desirability of rehabilitation measures that can be continued after release. In recent years the use of Section 34 of the Correctional Treatment Act of 1975 has increased, partly because of the fear of HIV and AIDS. Section 34 declares that a criminal drug user shall have the opportunity of serving his/her prison term in a therapeutic community programme or while submitting to a programme of family care in the framework of the parole system. Section 34 treatment can, and often does, continue after the date on which the prison sentence would have ended.

In some prisons, special drug treatment units have been set up. Offenders sentenced to long-term imprisonment have the option of moving to these institutional drug-free programmes. The oldest and most sophisticated internal drug-free programme is the Österaker project which started in 1978 at the closed national prison in Österaker near Stockholm. It is still the most comprehensive programme available. The project is developed in five units with a total of 60 places, with access to an additional 15 places for release-preparation or entry into the semi-open prison at Bögesund. Prisoners apply to enter the programme and are expected to stay for at least 8 months. If accepted, they have to sign a contract to follow the treatment plan worked out for each individual which includes daily urine sampling. In general, the programme can be compared in many ways with those provided in therapeutic communities, though modified to meet the special circumstances of detention. Daily life training, with an occupational or study component and a spare time component, constitute the basic treatment structure. After a stay of 8–24 months, inmates are prepared for an open prison, an outside treatment programme or a foster family project.

In recent years, five other national prisons have established so-called drug-free units, operating broadly according to therapeutic community principles. Four local prisons have, in conjunction with a research project, developed special programmes for reducing drug misuse in prison. Staff have been specially trained in matters concerning drug problems. Some other penal institutions have managed to separate some cells, to guarantee a drug-free milieu for inmates who want to avoid any contact with active drug-abusing fellow inmates. There are also two small units in one of the national prisons specially intended for motivating hard-core drug abusers who are unwilling to enter treatment during imprisonment or to go into treatment after their detention. In all these situations, the urine testing of inmates has been used intensively. An ambitious training programme for all prison staff has been developed in recent years. External experts are sometimes called in as advisers, however, and to run special activities such as group counselling and motivation.

Non-voluntary Treatment

France
In the mid-1980s, the drug situation in France at the social and political level deteriorated: the issue became increasingly political, sentences for drug users were toughened and repression, especially of retail drug dealers, increased. In 1986, the delicate balance in the prison system between assistance and control and between voluntary and non-voluntary conditions was upset when the Government proposed the so-called Chalandon Law. Apart from the prolonging of prison sentences and a general weakening of the position of inmates, this legal project provided for the non-voluntary treatment of drug abusers, for example at the request of their families, and the foundation of special and separate detention sites for drug abusers. The Chalandon project caused an unprecedented uproar in the professional (especially the medical) world. Medical and psychological objections to the concept of non-voluntary treatment were brought into the debate. These objections were specifically:

— the ambiguity of the concept of non-voluntary treatment, since people go to prison because of crimes they have committed and not because they are motivated to receive treatment;

22

— it is possible to detoxify people in prison, but treatment entails much more than detoxification since to be successful it also requires motivation;

— any treatment of drug dependence should be individually designed and prison, of all potential treatment settings, is the least suited to this individualization.

Another objection was that the French model of dealing with drug dependence was endangered: every country has its special history and present circumstances that form a coherent whole. It is counterproductive, generally speaking, to take out or bring in one element from a foreign debate; changes that aim at improving a particular system or model should take the whole of the debate into account. Finally, after much political struggle, the Government abandoned the part of the project that introduced non-voluntary treatment. The plans for building eight prison units for a total of 200 drug abusers, however, are being put into operation.

Federal Republic of Germany
A wide range of approaches has been developed in order to stimulate drug users to enter treatment. The level of coercion differs from one approach to another. Since 1982, the *Betäubungs-mittelgesetz* (the Law on psychotropic and narcotic substances) has enabled the courts to send criminal drug users with a remaining sentence of less than two years into treatment instead of having to stay in prison (*Therapie statt Strafe* — therapy instead of penalty). Since the drug user has to agree, it is not actually non-voluntary treatment, but it is mentioned here because of the German context. The prognosis for the treatment does not have to be good. The agencies that carry out treatment simply have a legal obligation to report to the court about the progress of the treatment or its premature termination. This was only one of the major contro-versial aspects of the law, especially among drug professionals. These professionals also criticized the pretence of a free choice between therapy and prison and in general the strong grip that government-linked professionals have on drug therapy. Other elements in this debate have been similar to the debate about the position of external drug counsellors in prison, discussed earlier. Since the criminal justice system has the money to subsidize treatment agencies and treatment agencies need a government permit, this resistance has finally broken down.

Options for real non-voluntary treatment come under the Criminal Procedures Act, which provides the possibility of non-voluntary observation in a mental hospital, and the provisions for treatment under the Criminal Code. Section 63 CC of the Criminal Code applies when people are not imputable and are inclined to serious criminal activities because of their mental condition. The time period of these measures is not defined. If a treatment order is made for drug abusers, their psychiatric condition is preponderant. Drug-dependent people can be treated (according to Section 64 CC) non-voluntarily in a mental hospital or in a specialized detoxification and treatment clinic, if drug dependence can be proven and if they can be expected to commit crimes. The maximum treatment period is two years and can be extended once. The treatment order can be carried out before, during or after detention. German drug professionals are generally very dissatisfied with the results of non-voluntary treatment in mental hospitals, particularly when no special drug-treatment unit is available, which is the case in most mental hospitals. In general, drug users are kept in closed wards. Specialized clinics have a better reputation. In the specialized clinics in Brauel (between Bremen and Hamburg) and Parsberg (in Bavaria), treatment is of a high quality with a highly individualized approach. A third clinic, Fronau in Berlin (West), was closed down quite some time ago.

After some years of experience, it can be concluded that the number of treatment orders under Sections 63 CC and 64 CC has decreased, and that most treatment comes under the *Betäubungsmittelgesetz*. Although a number of people are sentenced to non-voluntary treatment, the present emphasis in treatment is on voluntary cooperation *(6)*.

Sweden
Sweden has a long tradition of fighting alcohol consumption through policy measures based on a strong temperance movement. The history of non-voluntary treatment for alcohol-dependent people goes back decades. The reaction of the Swedish Government to drug use has essentially been the same as its reaction to alcohol use. Non-voluntary treatment for both drug- and alcohol-dependent people is regulated by the same law, *Lag om vard av missbrukare i vissa fall* (Law on care of drug abusers in certain cases, the LVM Law), passed by Parliament after 10 years of discussion. These discussions centred mainly on the responsibility of society to individuals regarding social, educational and medical

issues. Non-voluntary treatment is integrated in the normal social and medical systems. This means that non-criminal drug abusers (including alcohol abusers) may face a court decision about non-voluntary treatment. Judges work closely with the assistance system that is responsible for carrying out the LVM Law. The maximum duration of treatment is established at two terms of two months, but a judge can repeat the number of treatment periods *ad infinitum*. People are eligible for treatment under the LVM Law when their use of alcohol or drugs seriously endangers their physical or mental health, or when they cause serious damage to others. The treatment has to be carried out as far as possible with the client's cooperation. Respect for the client's privacy and self-determination should be the basis of treatment. Part of the LVM Law is also aimed at the non-voluntary treatment of people under 18 years of age.

The LVM treatment, in fact, has a very bad reputation in Sweden. Treatment generally takes place in special LVM houses, designed and equipped more for the physical care of skid row alcoholics than for the treatment of dependency. Recently, some new LVM treatment centres have been opened especially for drug abusers. With their focus on links with the voluntary treatment system their results seem to be better.

Two possible positive effects of the LVM Law are, however, that it can be, and is increasingly being, used to put pressure on individuals to enter voluntary treatment, and it can be used to remove addicted persons from their families if they threaten family life. These effects are possible mainly because of the integration of the LVM Law into normal social and medical care. Neighbourhood social workers, the school psychologist, the child-care agency and others can start the procedure for application of the LVM Law. Family doctors generally have the legal obligation to notify the authorities about an alcohol or drug-dependent person *(7)*.

United States
The role of the criminal justice system in society differs greatly between western European countries and the United States. In general, the position of the criminal justice system in American society is much more important, as is the impact of drug use on this system. For example, in New York State alone, by the end of 1987, some 40 763 people were detained, and for the first time the number of inmates who were in detention for drug-related offences

surpassed those imprisoned for any other crime. Furthermore, voluntary urine tests from more than 2000 men arrested by local police in 12 major cities indicated that 50–75% of these men were taking drugs. The criminal justice system is less likely to initiate the development of treatment programmes and a treatment structure in most European nations. As a consequence, the starting points for and the debate about non-voluntary treatment in Europe are different from those in the United States.

In the United States, experience with the non-voluntary treatment of drug-dependent people has been gathered over many years. In the early stage of the drug epidemic, a number of initiatives showed a close relationship between the criminal justice and the drug treatment systems. Federal treatment for drug-dependent people began with two Public Health Service drug treatment hospitals — first called farms — that opened in Lexington, Kentucky, in 1935 and in Fort Worth, Texas, in 1938. These facilities were designed primarily for the non-voluntary treatment of federal prisoners, but voluntary patients (under no legal pressure) were also accepted. Once withdrawn from drugs, most voluntary patients did not remain for the extended treatment programme. The treatment techniques used in these hospitals included individual and group counselling, vocational rehabilitation and a variety of other services focused on rehabilitation and re-entry into the community (8). These programmes were designed to treat not only withdrawal but also the drug-using habit and associated mental and social problems. The treatment programmes included four elements: drug withdrawal, residence in a drug-free environment, psychotherapy and supervised activities.

These early non-voluntary treatment experiments were not very successful. Follow-up studies from Lexington indicated an extremely high relapse rate, but also that conventional parole could be useful in keeping treated drug users from using drugs again. The most significant variable in determining abstinence in the confirmed user was the availability of compulsory parole supervision (9). Other studies further validated the importance of parole in drug-dependence treatment: for example, Brill & Lieberman reported that the use of authority derived from the judicial system was the single most important factor in the treatment of drug-dependent people (10). McGlothlin et al. reported from a 7-year follow-up study that close supervision, which included urine testing of ex-drug-dependent criminal offenders placed on

26

parole, produced lower rates of daily narcotic use, drug dealing and other criminal activity than did parole without testing or supervision *(11)*. Further follow-up data suggest that civil commitment, if used rationally, can be an effective approach for reducing drug use *(12)*. A review of follow-up studies from the Lexington and Fort Worth Public Health Service hospitals, however, suggests that treatment with legal coercion when combined with compulsory community follow-up produces better outcomes, although they were not vastly different from outcomes among voluntary patients *(13)*.

The Narcotic Addict Rehabilitation Act (NARA) was enacted in the United States at the federal level in 1966. NARA provided for supervised aftercare following hospitalization in Lexington and Fort Worth. NARA established a close link between the health care system and the criminal justice system. The programme provided civil commitment to keep drug abusers in treatment beyond withdrawal. It also included community-based follow-up care, after the detoxification provided initially at the Lexington and Fort Worth hospitals. Later, NARA inpatient treatment facilities were established in several major cities. NARA also set the stage for the community treatment of drug-dependent people by providing initial funding and by developing a group of drug-dependence treatment experts.

The NARA experience suggests that civil commitment will hold only about one third of drug-dependent people in treatment. This high drop-out rate may have been related to the intensive psychosocial approach. In addition, disruptive and non-compliant patients were found unsuitable for treatment and were quickly released. Maddux suggests that civil commitment is useful for bringing drug users into treatment, but it cannot overcome deficits in the treatment or ensure that patients participate in it *(13)*.

A third major American effort in the drug-dependence criminal justice area is the treatment alternatives to street crime (TASC) programme, which was established in 1972. Currently, more than 100 sites in 18 states have TASC programmes. They act as an outreach, or case-finding, function for treatment agencies, and as a bridge between the criminal justice system and the drug treatment programmes. The TASC programme identifies, assesses, refers and monitors appropriate drug- or alcohol-dependent non-violent offenders. Thus treatment serves as an alternative or supplement to the criminal justice system. Research suggests that the TASC link provides a less costly alternative to detention, and TASC clients remain in treatment longer. Perhaps most important to the success of TASC is the case management aspect which tracks the drug users through their drug careers *(14)*.

United States research suggests that treatment for drug dependence is effective. Clients entering drug-free outpatient counselling programmes, drug-free residential treatment and methadone maintenance treatment generally experience dramatic reductions in drug use and associated criminality. Many studies also show improvement in employment status and other behavioural outcomes. The question of which type of treatment is best becomes clouded by the fact that most clients have had experience of various types of treatment, often in more than one type of programme, before becoming abstinent. A treatment outcome prospective study (TOPS) included 12 000 clients in 10 American cities; five of those cities also had TASC programmes. Criminal justice referrals accounted for over 30% of the referrals to residential and outpatient drug-free programmes, and less than 3% of the referrals to outpatient methadone programmes. TOPS data indicate that criminal justice referrals were effective for many drug users at an early stage in their drug careers *(14)*.

The following consensus recommendations for the non-voluntary treatment of drug-dependent people were developed by a group of independent experts who met at the National Institute on Drug Abuse in January 1987 *(15)*.

It is recommended that the term ''compulsory treatment'' be used rather than ''civil commitment'' to capture a wider range of possible interventions, since civil commitment is only one type of compulsory treatment. Further, it is essential that candidates for compulsory treatment receive appropriate legal protections.

While there was considerable discussion, it was tentatively agreed that the type of persons targeted for compulsory treatment should be chronic drug abusers and, more specifically, the drug-abusing offender who would benefit most from treatment. Since it will not be possible to treat everyone who is identified or tests positive for drugs, it will be necessary to examine drug abuse careers and, initially, choose those intravenous drug abusers who pose the greatest threat to themselves and the community.

Treatment has proven effective in reducing drug abuse and, most specifically, in reducing intravenous drug abuse. Nonetheless, drug-dependence is chronic, and repeated interventions will probably be needed for most clients.

Research has shown that the length of time in treatment is related to treatment success and that long-term client aftercare and monitoring is an essential part of treatment. In addition, research has indicated that compulsory treatment in the form of civil commitment increases treatment retention for intravenous drug abusers.

Urine testing is an important tool for identifying and monitoring drug use for both the criminal justice system and treatment programs.

The efficacy of methadone treatment needs to be more clearly presented to personnel in the criminal justice system, since there seems to be a bias against methadone as a treatment approach.

The TC [therapeutic community] has a unique role for clients receiving long-term mandatory treatment and should remain an attractive treatment alternative for the judicial system.

[...]

The criminal justice system is important for client identification and retention. A strong link needs to be developed at all levels between treatment programs and the criminal justice system. The interface involves education, development of common goals, and inclusion of criminal justice as treatment items in data systems.

Compulsory treatment cannot be considered a panacea for dealing with the AIDS problem among intravenous drug abusers. Consideration also must be given to other alternatives for curbing the spread of AIDS infection ...

Conclusions

Although the effectiveness of non-voluntary treatment remains to be proved, there are some indications that it can be of value. Such treatment seems to be a rather successful part of the US model of treating drug dependence. This is different from the situation in western Europe, where no really successful experiences with non-voluntary treatment have been reported.

The concept of non-voluntary treatment, however, seems to fit better in some countries' models (e.g. the Federal Republic of Germany and Sweden) than it does in others (e.g. France, but also Belgium, the Netherlands and Switzerland). This consideration, and the professional and social debate that is being triggered by proposals that affect key elements of a country's drug assistance model, seem to advise against implementing one country's drug policy in another country's very different circumstances.

Treatment of drug abusers'
other health problems

When speaking of the health problems of drug-dependent people in prison, three different value systems are evident: the criminal justice system, the health system and the dependency system. The systems can be drawn as circles that are both moving and overlapping. The movement and the overlap have become stronger in the past few years, and the conflict of values between the systems grows in particular because of AIDS, but also because of the following situations. In many European countries, the criminal justice system and prisons more specifically are in the midst of a serious crisis, partly because of overcrowding, lack of general hygiene (e.g. in the United Kingdom) and uncontrolled growth (e.g. in France and the Netherlands). Furthermore, there is a lack of independence and quality among health care staff in prisons who are often appointed by and answerable to prison authorities (e.g. in the United Kingdom, where they are subject to the Official Secrets Act) instead of to their own professional and ethical standards.

Drug users accumulate personal, social and medical handicaps, because of the underlying difficulties that led to their initiation (personality disorders, family and other social problems, psychiatric pathology); social and economic problems such as unemployment, poverty, debts, and homelessness; problems with the criminal justice system including harassment by the police, repeated arrests, and prison sentences for repeated minor offences, drug trafficking and occasionally more serious crimes; and health problems such as hepatitis, abscesses, septicaemia, overdoses, suicide attempts, and AIDS *(16)*.

31

AIDS and HIV

Present situation

Whereas the homosexual community experiences the AIDS epidemic as a dramatic threat to their existence as a relatively well integrated and socially functioning group, intravenous drug users appear to view AIDS as "just one more problem" to add to their burdens. A young drug user already faces the risk of death through overdose, hepatitis or septicaemia. He or she often faces an existence dominated by marginality and discrimination. AIDS reinforces a condemnatory public image and brings yet another prospect of suffering and death to those whose personal tragedies have already led them to harm their own bodies and regularly to risk death.

The experience of counselling drug users about AIDS is therefore fundamentally different from that among homosexuals or in the general population. This fact is most evident in prisons. The ambivalence and the implicit failure of the prison to respond to drug dependence creates an unpromising background for facing the realities of the AIDS epidemic. Prison creates mistrust, tension, humiliation, uncertainty and personal devaluation. The stress of being in prison produces frequent reactive states of anxiety, depression and suicide attempts, significantly more often than in the general population. Yet it is in prison that a significant part of the AIDS epidemic is occurring and must be faced, because of the high incidence of drug users in European prisons. By statistical extrapolation from data on the seropositivity of intravenous drug users in prison populations, it is clear that many prison populations have a higher rate of seropositivity than any other group. This conclusion is confirmed by epidemiological observations within prisons. It would be wrong, however, to condemn prisons as breeding grounds for AIDS, since the risks of getting infected are especially high in outside society, where control of the main risk behaviour, drug injection and sexual intercourse, is generally much less than in prison. For the United States, there is evidence that AIDS is increasing more slowly in prisons than in the population as a whole *(17)*. European experts are generally of the same opinion, although scientific data are not yet available.

A coherent AIDS control strategy

AIDS cases now occur regularly within prisons and the numbers will certainly rise in the years to come. Prison medical services and hospitals are not equipped to cope with this emerging problem. It is clear therefore that a coherent strategy is needed to deal with AIDS within prisons. This strategy should respond adequately to the public health aspects, by limiting the spread of the epidemic both within prison and following release, through sexual contact, by intravenous contamination or by pregnancy; and to the human aspects, by preventing irrational fear and panic among staff and prisoners, leading to segregation and discrimination, by providing counselling and support to seropositive inmates, and by giving high quality care under humane conditions to inmates who develop AIDS.

A survey carried out in 17 countries, on behalf of the Council of Europe, shows how prison doctors and administrators have reacted to the AIDS epidemic in ways that are not always scientifically and ethically sound. The pressing need to control HIV infection in prison and to develop a coherent strategy within a closed, authoritarian environment poses a serious challenge to prison medical staff. It is far from certain that sufficient resources and professional independence will be available to cope. Failure to react adequately to the epidemic in prisons, however, would have serious consequences both for the community as a whole and for the ethical position of prison medical staff *(18)*.

A major factor to be taken into account in the development of a coherent strategy is the diversity of individual responses among drug-using inmates:

— some inmates ask for HIV counselling and screening while others prefer not to know;

— some prisoners react to a positive test result with relative equanimity, while others have acute reactions of distrust and disbelief which may relate to its effect on their personal experience, such as their life expectancy, sexual relationships, and possibility of having children;

— few drug abusers who are seronegative seem motivated to stop drug use, although they appear to accept the idea of using clean injection equipment and (sometimes) less dangerous ways of administering drugs;

— seropositive inmates sometimes express antisocial reactions, e.g. by refusing to consider using precautions in sexual relationships or in prostitution; in extreme cases the possibility of contagion may be used as a threat, for example by biting when frustrated or angry.

Special significance of AIDS in prison

The transmission routes of HIV are limited, so the natural bound-aries of the epidemic are set by patterns of human behaviour. On the other hand, bridging groups and bridging behaviour do exist, allowing HIV infection to be passed from one group to another by:

— homosexual men who also use drugs intravenously and share injection equipment;

— bisexual men with (frequent) contacts with both sexes;

— male and female intravenous drug users who engage in prostitution;

— heterosexual men who frequent prostitutes, especially from high-risk areas such as Central Africa and some Latin American countries;

— induced homosexual behaviour in prison.

The bridging phenomenon appears to have gained ground over the past few years. A most disquieting development is that the number of people who are seropositive is rising steeply in the intravenous drug-using communities of many, though not all, countries and the epidemic is thus beginning to escape from its previously rather watertight compartments.

Prisons may well occupy a key position for the control of AIDS in the community. They provide bridging situations where con-siderable numbers of intravenous drug users — a high proportion of whom are probably infected with HIV — may continue to use drugs intravenously and to share needles, and can be expected to have occasional homosexual contacts. The frequency of intra-venous drug use and the frequency and type of homosexual con-tacts in prison are unknown but anecdotal accounts by prisoners suggest that anal intercourse and oral/genital sex are rather fre-quent, even between inmates who have a heterosexual orientation outside prison. Thus, induced homosexual behaviour in prison provides a bridge between a known high-risk group (intravenous drug users) and individuals who are generally not at high risk.

The fact that it is possible to impose much stricter controls in prison than in the general community, has led to suggestions that strict controls should be imposed to limit the spread of HIV. Such a policy would imply compulsory HIV testing of all prisoners. This paternalistic approach can be defended by arguing that prison authorities have a direct responsibility to protect prisoners from the consequences of promiscuity since the possibility of homosexual rape in prisons is real. Nevertheless, there is a clear impression that those who advocate the routine compulsory screening of prisoners are seeking a scapegoat group for political reasons. If homosexual rape is a significant risk in prisons, this is an argument for improving human conditions for prisoners and staff-to-prisoner ratios, for decreasing overcrowding and for providing activities, rather than for imposing compulsory screening with no safeguards for confidentiality.

For both practical and ethical reasons, measures for the control of HIV and AIDS in the prison environment should closely follow the strategy for the community as a whole. This implies an approach stressing individual responsibility in which each prisoner is treated as being autonomous and personally responsible for his or her own health and the consequences of his or her behaviour. This means informing inmates about AIDS risks and giving them opportunities to take prophylactic measures. The earlier policy of focusing preventive advice on seropositive prisoners is no longer adequate. All prisoners are now concerned by the risk of HIV and they should receive counselling that is valid not only for the duration of their imprisonment but also after their release.

Recommended control measures

The following concrete measures are needed to control HIV infection in prisons and to prevent unnecessary alarm and inappropriate measures by staff or prisoners.

(*a*) Information should be provided to all prison staff on AIDS and other communicable diseases. This information should be regularly updated.

(*b*) Prisoners should receive written information adapted to their intellectual and cultural levels (e.g. not using medical terminology, and translated for foreigners) about HIV/AIDS, and particularly about the risks of homosexual contacts in prison and about intravenous drug use.

(*c*) Condoms should be made available on request to prisoners who have any opportunity for homosexual contacts in prison, and

35

also before temporary and final release. It is recognized that in some countries condom distribution is still considered to be a taboo subject and that sometimes condoms are simply forbidden in prisons (e.g. the United Kingdom).

(*d*) Active steps should be taken to prevent the illicit introduction into and use of injection equipment in prison. All prisoners should receive detailed information about avoiding the use of dirty injection material. If needles and syringes are legally available in society, prison authorities should consider the distribution of clean injection equipment in prison by the medical services and under medical secrecy. (In Switzerland, for instance, a controlled experiment of giving out sterile drug-injection equipment in a high security prison has been carried out.)

(*e*) HIV tests should be made available on request to all inmates. Pre- and post-test counselling is essential to prepare prisoners for receiving the results in an environment where normal social support is lacking. The results should be communicated to the prisoner by medical staff. The prison administration and judicial authorities should not be informed of the results unless the prisoner specifically asks for this to be done. Psychological support should be available for HIV-positive prisoners.

(*f*) The isolation and segregation of seropositive drug users is not justified and may be counterproductive. Such prisoners can work in all settings, including prison kitchens.

(*g*) General hygienic standards and good nutrition should be available to all prisoners, since these factors may have a prophylactic effect on the development of AIDS in those who are seropositive. Paradoxically, the AIDS epidemic may force the criminal justice and prison authorities to improve the overall standards of hygiene and health care in the prison system, for both prisoners and staff.

(*h*) Adequate measures for the care of AIDS patients and of prisoners dying from AIDS must be taken by providing sufficient human resources and treatment facilities, possibly including the prescription of zidovudine. Suspended sentences or pardon should be considered when prisoners are diagnosed as AIDS patients or during the last stages of their illness.

Conclusion

With the AIDS epidemic drug abusers become an even greater problem than before for the prison system. Alternative responses to the antisocial behaviour associated with drug dependence must be sought. For humanitarian, therapeutic and public health reasons, more understanding and tolerance is needed of drug use and drug dependence, both in prisons and in the community. AIDS has particularly highlighted the vulnerability of drug users in society. The epidemiological realities of the epidemic show that despite marginalization drug users are an integral part of society. By showing drug users at risk, people who are seropositive and those who develop AIDS that they have the right to the same level of prevention, of care and of consideration, society can demonstrate in concrete terms its commitment to understanding, human care and integration.

Suicidal Behaviour

Relation between drug abuse and suicidal behaviour

The relation between drug abuse and suicidal behaviour is close, both technically and with regard to the personalities involved. This relation, and the consideration that HIV infection and AIDS may induce suicidal behaviour during imprisonment, are reasons for giving some special attention to the subject.

The focus here is on parasuicide, which is the better alternative term for what is usually called attempted suicide. In recent decades it has become increasingly clear that most people who deliberately injure or poison themselves, even in the heat of the moment, are aware of the fact that they have a fair chance of surviving because they are not attempting suicide. If asked why they injured themselves their answers fall into three general categories:

— the cry for help ("I wanted to show how miserable I felt", "I wanted to let them feel how they mistreated me", etc.);

— the wish for temporary interruption of consciousness ("I wanted to stop these thoughts", "I wanted to have some rest", etc.);

— the wish to die.

To summarize, most people who deliberately injure themselves have an ambiguous orientation towards life and death; they do not want to live the life they live but neither do they want to die. For this reason, the term suicide attempt is really off the mark; the word parasuicide is more apt.

It might appear that parasuicide would include drug dependence. The difference, however, is that drug dependence is a habitual behaviour while an act must be non-habitual to be considered parasuicide. As previously stated, however, the relation is very close, particularly since both drug use and parasuicide are ways to cope with pain or stress, and both are dangerous. Moreover, drugs, including tranquillizers and other psychoactive drugs, are used as a method of parasuicide. Even people who are not using these drugs on a regular basis tend to commit parasuicide by taking overdoses. Apart from the phenomenological relation there is a statistical one: many persons who commit (para)suicide have a history of drug or alcohol dependence; drug and alcohol dependence are important predictors of suicidal behaviour. Drug-dependent people are significantly more likely to commit parasuicide than non-dependent people. Unfortunately, many drug overdoses are not recognized as (para)suicides.

Two other arguments that relate to drug dependence and suicidal behaviour should be mentioned. First, many depressions in drug users are likely to be caused by known secondary drug problems — social, legal, psychological, health and financial troubles, loss of self-esteem, loss of physical and intellectual abilities, AIDS, and loss of respect and love. All these secondary effects of drug dependence may foster depression and suicidal feelings. Second, both drug dependence and suicidal behaviour are likely to be caused by some third factor, such as proneness to depression or other mental disorders. Social conditioning can affect the choice between these types of behaviour: in many countries, more men turn to drugs while more women turn to parasuicide.

Thus, imprisonment can increase a person's proneness to parasuicide, because:

— it fosters stress;

— it generally means abstinence from drugs, at least for some time, and thus loss of the ability to cope;

— it often means confronting a multitude of problems.

38

Predictors and preventive measures

The prediction and prevention of parasuicide are important and they are to a certain extent quite possible. The following predictors of suicidal behaviour and preventive measures are worth mentioning; most of the measures can be implemented without much extra expense. The first three apply to everyone, the next three are specific to prisoners.

Predictor. If a person has committed one or more parasuicides the risk of another parasuicide is increased; the more prior parasuicides, the higher the risk of suicide.

Preventive measures. Prison staff often do not know if an inmate has a history of overdoses/parasuicides. Information, for example between prisons and police, is not systematically exchanged, and staff are not accustomed to asking inmates for information. The prediction and prevention of parasuicides can be improved by dedicating attention to this topic, by exchanging information, and by more specific intake screening.

Predictor. If a person is considering parasuicide, he or she will often try to communicate his/her feelings to others, especially when dangerous methods are contemplated such as hanging or jumping, or if detailed suicide plans have been made. The common idea that people who talk about suicide will not do it is false. Most people do give indications, directly or more covertly, for example by giving away their personal belongings.

Preventive measures. Personnel should be trained to pay attention to this type of suicidal communication and should not hesitate to inquire. In fact, speaking about his/her suicidal feelings will often be a relief for the inmate. Staff, unfortunately, often feel threatened or manipulated by suicidal communication and show a tendency to ignore the seriousness of an inmate's plans.

Predictor. Depression is another indicator of suicidal risk and is the most common form of mental disorder seen in suicidal patients. Symptoms such as sleeplessness, loss of appetite, self-isolation, anxiety and feelings of hopelessness and helplessness suggest severe depression.

Preventive measures. Several instruments can reliably measure depression and suicide risk, but they do not yet seem to be used systematically in prisons. It may be worth while to introduce, and possibly to reassess these instruments in prison situations.

Predictor. The risk of committing (para)suicide is highest during the first days and weeks of detention.

Preventive measures. Special attention should be paid to this first stage of detention. A psychological screening should be part of the prison intake process. In some cases, it may be wise to prepare entering inmates for the stress and despair they may have to suffer and to learn how to cope in non-destructive ways.

Predictor. Inmates who commit (para)suicide have a relatively high level of consumption of prescribed drugs, mostly sedatives.

Preventive measures. Care must be taken when prescribing drugs, especially without additional therapy. Moreover, since the timing of (para)suicide is often connected with external events, such as judicial hearings, or letters (or no more letters) from the family and others, staff should pay attention to such events.

Predictor. Inmates who face long prison sentences and who have committed heavily sanctioned crimes are more suicidal than other inmates. Sexual offenders, who are despised not only by the general public but also by their fellow inmates, are at particularly high risk. Actually, all inmates who are not only isolated from family and friends, but also isolated in the prison population, are more likely to become suicidal. Dutch research has shown that foreign inmates account for half of all parasuicides in prison *(19)*.

Preventive measures. Special attention by well trained staff is most important. Currently, the standard institutional reaction to parasuicide or the risk of parasuicide is to place the inmate in an isolation cell. This measure, which aims at preventing the inmate from injuring himself or herself, will often make the inmate more desperate. Isolating an inmate is a measure only for extreme cases and in all these cases consultation with a mental health professional is required.

Other Health Problems and Preventive Measures

Many drug abusers are admitted to prison in a very poor state of dental health. Dental care could well be provided during a prison stay and might help to build up confidence in the treating staff. Hepatitis B vaccination on admission would be a useful preventive measure. In the days and weeks following release, the risk of opiate overdose increases among opiate abusers whose tolerance level has been lowered by enforced abstinence. A special warning about this possibility should be given.

Research priorities

Since research and its results have limited influence on policy-making and management, it is important to introduce the idea of the applicability of research findings. Research projects that are geared to this generally have much more impact. Taking this into account, the following research topics may be identified as priorities.

Basic issues
Basic issues for investigation include: the factors determining the reasons and motivation of drug users for becoming and staying involved in drug use, stopping their behaviour, and entering into and staying in treatment. The effects and influence of detention also deserve study, particularly with regard to health problems associated with drug use, the motivation to enter treatment, and inmates in general, both drug users and non-users. Studies on HIV and AIDS in prison should examine the relevance and practice of HIV-testing, and HIV/AIDS education, control and treatment measures. Another important topic is (para)suicide in prison with the focus on prevention.

Concepts and terminology
Priority should be given to the development of adequate frameworks to enable the comparison of various research designs and research methods used in different national and international situations, related especially to concepts such as compulsion, coercion, pressure and voluntarism. Studies should examine the relationship between drug use/drug dependence and suicidal behaviour. A reliable instrument should be developed to assess the suicide risk in prisoners.

Epidemiology
Studies should be conducted on:

— offenders with drug-related problems in prison, developing and using comparable research frameworks such as Casselman's study *(2)*;

— the prevalence and incidence of HIV;

— the incidence of (para)suicide, not only in prisons but also in police cells.

Client characteristics
Psychometric research should determine a profile of drug-dependent persons/inmates. Research should be aimed at improving the matching of inmates/clients with prisons/treatment programmes.

Evaluation
Important evaluative research should include:

— studies to help institutions give content and form to the facilities/programme elements they are implementing;

— studies on the effects of certain programme elements or methods;

— cost-effectiveness studies on different levels, from element to programme.

A distinction between the types of research required might be made: abuser-oriented and institution-oriented. The first type would preferably be longitudinal and could then study the role of detention in the life of the drug abuser. The second would focus on the effects that drug abuse treatment programmes have on the community. Research is needed also on the links between institutes in the health and judicial systems and should study the movements between treatment and detention. Newman & Price refer to this as "service-delivery research" *(20)*.

Finally, it must be stressed that all research must be set up in such a way that all groups who are interested can reap the benefit.

Conclusions and recommendations

Medical Care

Health and medical care should be provided for all prisoners who enter the criminal justice system, most specifically in prisons. Medical care for prisoners in some countries does not reach the same level as medical care for the general population.

In the context of WHO's global strategy of health for all by the year 2000, prisoners should have the right to receive health care equivalent to that provided for the country's general population and governed by the same ethical principles, including confidentiality and informed consent.

There may be a specific need to warn drug abusers about the dangers of overdosing immediately upon release from prison.

A structure should be created to promote cooperation between health and prison authorities.

Medical care and health care in prisons should make available specific services focused on: drug detoxification, internal medicine, dental care, psychiatric care, psychological care, social services, and surgical care (e.g. removal of tattoos).

All medical professionals and services should cooperate in proper and responsible prescribing practices.

Treatment of Drug Dependence

The motivation to enter treatment should be examined to determine the optimal approach for specific groups of individuals.

Prison is not generally a therapeutic environment, and there is an apparent contradiction between treatment and imprisonment for

44

drug users. Although people must be imprisoned for their crimes, treatment should be made available in the prison system for those who desire it.

Drug dependence is a chronic relapsing disease and treatment programmes must include the possibility of assistance at any point in the drug abuser's life. If possible, prison should be used as a setting in which to begin the initial drug-dependence treatment process.

Drug-dependence treatment consists of many levels of interaction including: counselling, behaviour modification, psychoanalysis, psychosocial interventions, educational and vocational training, etc. It should be stressed, however, that these types of treatment have not been developed for use in situations such as prison, and their effect may depend on a certain freedom on the part of the client to experience the progress he or she is making during treatment.

When the levels of freedom and coercion are examined, and the different forms of drug treatment that exist as part of the prison system are taken into account, a simple distinction between voluntary and non-voluntary treatment is not adequate. A more sophisticated definition of both voluntary and non-voluntary elements is needed in all the forms of treatment that exist in the criminal justice system.

Although no clear consensus could be reached by the meeting on this subject, it was suggested that a definition be developed based on two objective dimensions or axes: (*i*) who is making the decision about treatment; and (*ii*) in what setting the treatment takes place.

Another suggestion was that a third dimension be introduced in this definition — the dimension of motivation. Motivation is a subjective and unmeasurable criterion, however, which is different from the decision-maker and the setting.

Since drug-dependence treatment should be directed at modifying lifestyles and should focus on developing a positive attitude towards the treatment process, a minimal level of motivation is required for any form of treatment. It should be noted that motivation is not a state of affairs but a process with many ups and downs including growth and relapse.

In many countries, there are short prison sentences that provide only limited opportunities for modifying lifestyles and for the subsequent reinforcement of behavioural change. Nevertheless, these situations provide an opportunity for cooperation with community settings, along with appropriate freedom, as a first step in a continuing treatment process.

Special Health Problems

HIV infection and AIDS are currently the most urgent special health problems for prisoners. The joint planning and interaction between the prison system and the general health care system are extremely important, especially now that intravenous drug abusers represent a substantial portion of the HIV-infected persons in several countries.

A country-specific AIDS policy should be developed for the criminal justice system. This policy should include a description of how to manage this special health problem, which includes persons who are HIV-positive and persons with AIDS.

In addition, it must be recognized that in a rapidly changing situation current facilities may not be adequate to cope with the AIDS epidemic. The financial strain that might be imposed by governments is uncertain. Thus, countries should use various approaches to contain the potential spread of AIDS in the prison system, which could include education and information, as well as provisions for safer sex.

Several principles should be followed in dealing with AIDS. HIV testing of prisoners should not be mandatory and, when HIV testing is used, appropriate pre- and post-test counselling with informed consent should be incorporated. Prisoners should be able to participate in AIDS-related treatment programmes such as those using zidovudine. If such treatment is started in prison, however, continuation and follow-up should be maintained in the community after release from prison. If appropriate, epidemiological studies, including HIV testing, could be useful in determining the incidence and prevalence of HIV infection in prisons, but this type of testing should be carried out anonymously.

It is recognized that suicidal behaviour is a complicating factor when drug-dependent people are imprisoned. The incidence of suicide and parasuicide in prison is several times higher than it is in the community, especially during the first weeks of detention, the period that coincides with detoxification. The early identification of people at high risk is a prerequisite for the prevention of suicidal behaviour. Previous parasuicides, suicidal communication, depression and social isolation are indicators of suicidal risk. An

46

environment in which suicidal feelings can be expressed will improve this identification. Recommended preventive measures are the education of staff, measures to diminish or remove isolation, and teaching inmates some basic skills for coping with stress.

Research Questions and Priorities

Research should be carried out in two main areas: treatment evaluation and motivation. The main treatment evaluation question is:

— What treatment approaches are being applied or could be used within the prison system?

Motivational questions and issues include:

— Since drug-dependent people form a very heterogeneous population, it appears necessary to assess the psychosocial and psychiatric state of every individual inmate. Diagnosis and prognosis are major research possibilities that are now being examined. The outcome of that research should be used to improve the selection and matching of clients to different kinds of prison and programme.

— Could detention by itself help change people's motivation to undergo treatment? In addition, are there elements or aspects of the prison environment that could be identified as having major influences on motivation?

— Does detention influence people's motivation to change their behaviour?

— The establishment of drug-dependence treatment interventions, including their psychological implications within the prison system, should be systematically evaluated.

— Longitudinal studies on drug-use careers should evaluate methods of motivating drug-dependent people to change their behaviour.

References

1. *Role of the criminal justice system in responding to the problems of drug misusers.* Strasbourg, Council of Europe, 1987.
2. **Casselman, J.** *Study of offenders with illicit drug-related problems in prison in five European countries.* Brussels, WHO Collaborating Centre for Health, Psychosocial and Psychobiological Factors, 1986.
3. *The Whitaker report.* Report of the Committee on Inquiry into the Penal System. Dublin, Stationery Office, 1985.
4. **Kaiser, G. et al.** *Strafvollzug — Eine Einführung in die Grundlagen.* Heidelberg/Karlsruhe, 1978.
5. **Kindermann, W.** *Was ist als Hilfe für Drogenabhängige im Strafvollzug durch Initiative von aussen machbar?* Unpublished working paper presented at the Symposium *"Therapie und/oder Strafe"*. Frankfurt am Main, 1981.
6. *Bericht der Bundesregierung über die Erfahrungen mit dem Gesetz zur Neuordnung des Betäubungsmittelrechts.* Bonn, Deutscher Bundestag, 1983.
7. **Sijes, M.B.** *Non-voluntary treatment of drug users in Western Germany and Sweden.* The Hague, Research and Documentation Centre of the Netherlands Ministry of Justice, 1987 (Justitiele Verkenningen).
8. **Leukefeld, C.G.** The clinical connection: drugs and crime. *International journal of the addictions,* **20**(6–7): 1049–1064 (1985).
9. **Vaillant, G.E.** A twelve-year follow-up of New York narcotic addicts. III. Some social and psychiatric characteristics. *Archives of general psychiatry,* **15**(6): 599–609 (1966).

10. **Brill, L. & Lieberman, L.** *Authority and addiction.* Boston, Little, Brown and Co., 1969.
11. **McGlothlin, W.H. et al.** *An evaluation of the California Civil Addict Program.* Rockville, MD, National Institute on Drug Abuse, 1977.
12. **Anglin, M.D.** The efficacy of civil commitment in treating narcotic addiction. *In*: Leukefeld, C.G. & Tims, F.M., ed. *Compulsory treatment of drug abuse: research and clinical practice.* Rockville, MD, National Institute on Drug Abuse, 1988 (NIDA Research Monograph 86).
13. **Maddux, J.F.** Clinical experience with civil commitment. *In*: Leukefeld, C.G. & Tims, F.M., ed. *Compulsory treatment of drug abuse: research and clinical practice.* Rockville, MD, National Institute on Drug Abuse, 1988 (NIDA Research Monograph 86).
14. **Hubbard, R.L. et al.** The criminal justice client in drug abuse treatment. *In*: Leukefeld, C.G. & Tims, F.M., ed. *Compulsory treatment of drug abuse: research and clinical practice.* Rockville, MD, National Institute on Drug Abuse, 1988 (NIDA Research Monograph 86).
15. **Leukefeld, C.G. & Tims, F.M.** Compulsory treatment: a review of findings. *In*: Leukefeld, C.G. & Tims, F.M., ed. *Compulsory treatment of drug abuse: research and clinical practice.* Rockville, MD, National Institute on Drug Abuse, 1988 (NIDA Research Monograph 86).
16. WHO Technical Report Series, No. 618, 1978 (Twenty-first report of the WHO Expert Committee on Drug Dependence).
17. *Washington post*, 10 May 1988.
18. **Harding, T.W.** AIDS in prison. *Lancet*, **II**: 1260–1263 (1987).
19. **Bernasco, W. et al.** *Zelfdestructief gedrag van gedetineerden* [Self-destructive behaviour by detainees]. Leiden, Department of Clinical and Health Psychology, Leiden University, 1986.
20. **Newman, C.L. & Price, B.R.** *Jails and treatment.* London, Sage, 1977.

Annex 1

Working papers

Non-voluntary treatment, *Odile Dormoy*

An exploration of nonvoluntary treatment for drug abusers, *C.G. Leukefeld*

Identification of drug users in prison and treatment measures at admission, *J. Casselman*

An evaluation of the effectiveness of correctional and supportive measures employed within the framework of the Swedish correctional and parole system in reducing risks of the spread of HIV among intravenous drug abusers, *R.W. Goldsmith & I. Östborn*

External drug-counselling in prisons, *A. Rosenberg*

Motivation towards treatment of addicted prisoners, *P.A. Roorda*

AIDS in prison, with special reference to drug dependence, *T.W. Harding*

Suicidal behaviour by detained drug abusers, *W. Bernasco*

Research priorities with regard to health problems of drug abusers in prison, *G.M. Schippers & L.H. Erkelens*

A study of psychological and social intervention factors in cases of prisoners with ''drug'' problems; an overall evaluation of their legal and judicial situation, *A.A. Gomes Leandro*

Annex 2

Participants

Temporary Advisers

Professor J. Ballesteros, University of the Basque Country, Vitoria, Spain

Professor J. Casselman, University Psychiatric Centre, Catholic University of Leuven, Bierbeek, Belgium

Dr Odile Dormoy, Médicin-chef, Service médico-psychologique régional du Centre pénitentiaire de Fleury-Merogis, Paris, France

Mr E. Engelsman, Head, Alcohol, Drugs and Tobacco Branch, Ministry of Welfare, Health and Cultural Affairs, Rijswijk, Netherlands

Mr L.H. Erkelens, Deputy Head, Research Office, Prison Administration, Ministry of Justice, The Hague, Netherlands

Dr T.W. Harding, University Institute of Legal Medicine, University Medical Centre, Geneva, Switzerland

Dr P. Knudsen, Consultant Physician, Herstedvester Prison, Albertslund, Denmark

Dr P. Lens, Acting Medical Director, Ministry of Justice, The Hague, Netherlands (*Chairman*)

Dr C.G. Leukefeld, Deputy Director, Division of Clinical Research, National Institute on Drug Abuse, Rockville, MD, USA

Mr A. Rosenberg, Wilhelminenstraße 8, Wiesbaden, Federal Republic of Germany

Dr G.M. Schippers, Associate Professor, Psychology Department, Catholic University, Nijmegen, Netherlands

Mr I. Östborn, Psychologist, Siriusgatan 17, Lund, Sweden

Observers

Mr W. Bernasco, Department of Clinical and Health Psychology, Leiden, Netherlands

Dr A.A. Gomes Leandro, Centre for Legal Studies, Lisbon, Portugal

Mr J. Puyol Pinuela, Administrative Officer, Pompidou Group, Council of Europe, Strasbourg, France

Dr P.A. Roorda, Special Adviser to the Ministry of Justice, Haarlem, Netherlands

Professor A. Springer, Director, Ludwig Boltzmann Institut für Suchtforschung, Vienna, Austria

Mr H. van Vliet, Zeeburgerpad t.o. 38, Amsterdam, Netherlands

WHO Regional Office for Europe

Mr C. Goos, Scientist, Abuse of Psychoactive Drugs

Drug abusers
in prisons

Managing their health problems

WHO Library Cataloguing in Publication Data

Drug abusers in prisons : managing their health problems : report on
a WHO meeting, The Hague, 16–18 May 1988

(WHO regional publications European series ; No.27)

1.Health services 2.Prisoners 3.Substance abuse
4.Europe I.Series

ISBN 92 890 1118 1   (NLM Classification: WM 270)
ISSN 0378-2255